Learn to Read

CW01261682

For Beginners

BOOK 1

By Stephanie Lipsey-Liu

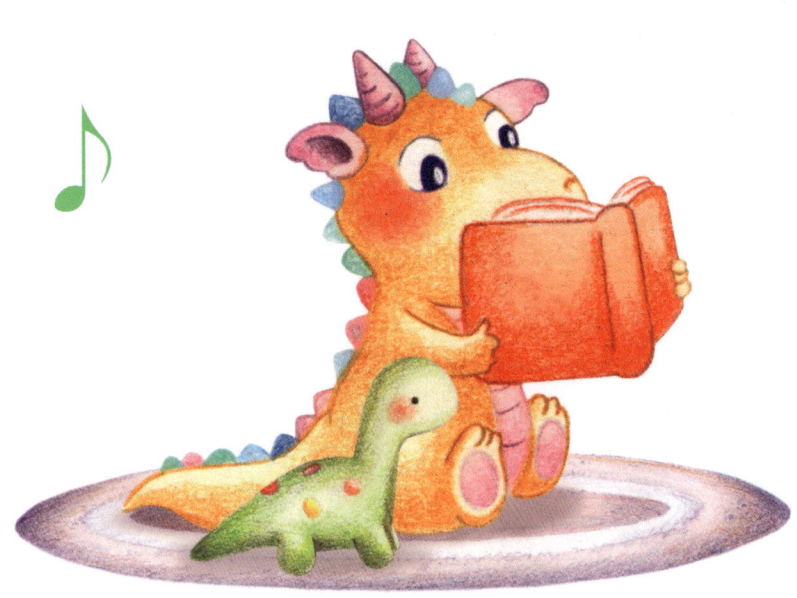

Note From The Author

Well done for taking the first step to being able to read music!

You'll have to put a bit of work in, but I've tried to make it as easy as possible!

Once you've mastered this book, see how you get on with Book 2 which will provide everything you need to know for your ABRSM Grade 1 Theory!

Steph

Contents

Page 1 Treble Clef Notes

Page 7 Bass Clef Notes

Page 13 Notes Outside The Lines

Page 17 Note and Rest Length

Page 19 Dotted Notes and Rests

Page 21 Time Signatures

Page 26 Musical Terms

Page 30 Answers

Page 35 Manuscript Paper

Copyright © 2024 by Stephanie Lipsey-Liu.
All rights reserved
No part of this publication may be reproduced or transmitted in any form or by any means, electronic or mechanical, including photocopying, recording, scanning or otherwise, or through any information browsing, storage or retrieval system, without permission in writing from the publisher.
First printed 2024 ISBN 978-1-917565-00-4

Little Lion Publishing UK
Nottingham, England
www.littlelionpublishing.co.uk

Treble Clef Notes

Starting at A at the bottom, the notes go up in alphabetical order from each line to each space. You may notice that once we get to G, we start again at A and carry on again to the next G.

The 5 main lines that the notes sit on, are called a stave or a staff. Middle C sits on one small line (ledger line) below the stave in the treble clef.

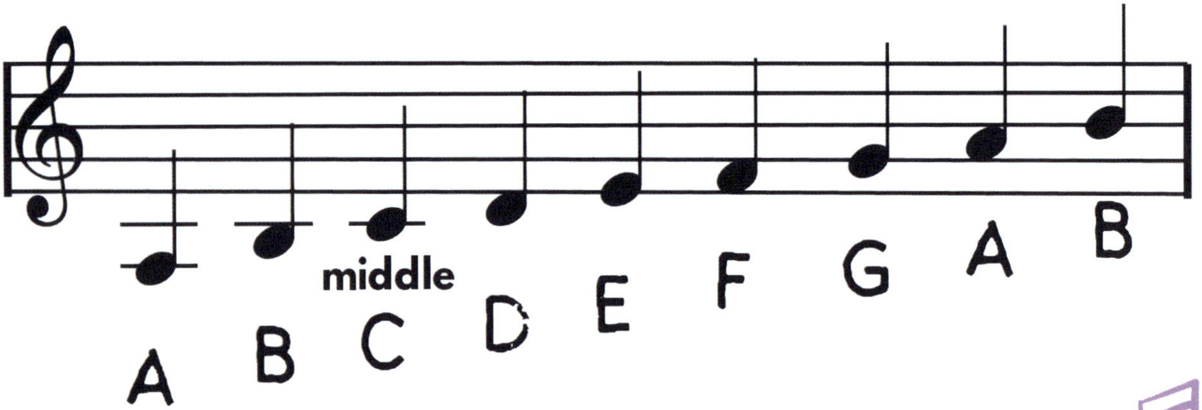

A B middle C D E F G A B

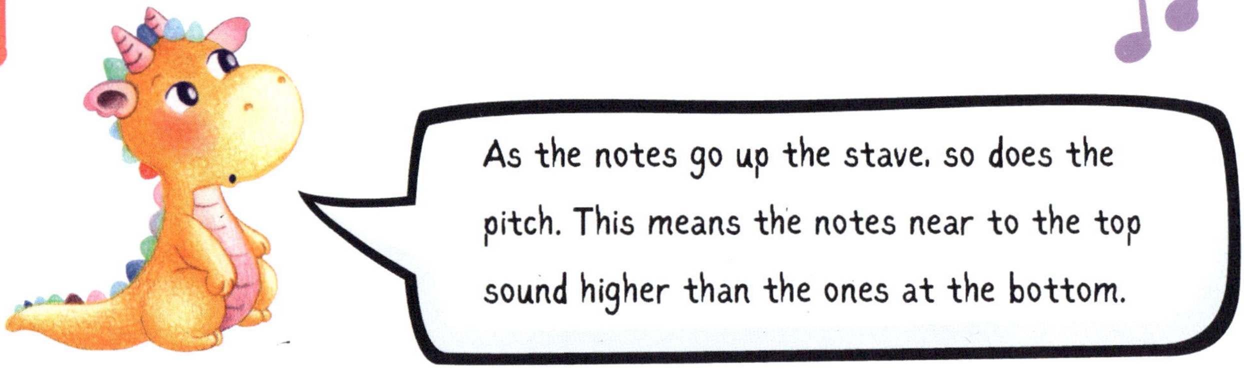

As the notes go up the stave, so does the pitch. This means the notes near to the top sound higher than the ones at the bottom.

1

The notes before the middle line have their sticks up and the notes above the middle line have their sticks down.

Below is the symbol for the treble clef.
It always curls around the second line from the bottom, the "G line".
Have a go at drawing some treble clefs below. Start by tracing the first ones then try on your own.

Treble Clef Notes

The Rhyme For The Lines

To help us remember the notes on each line, we can learn the rhyme on the blackboard.

The letter at the beginning of each word is the note for each line, starting from the bottom to the top.

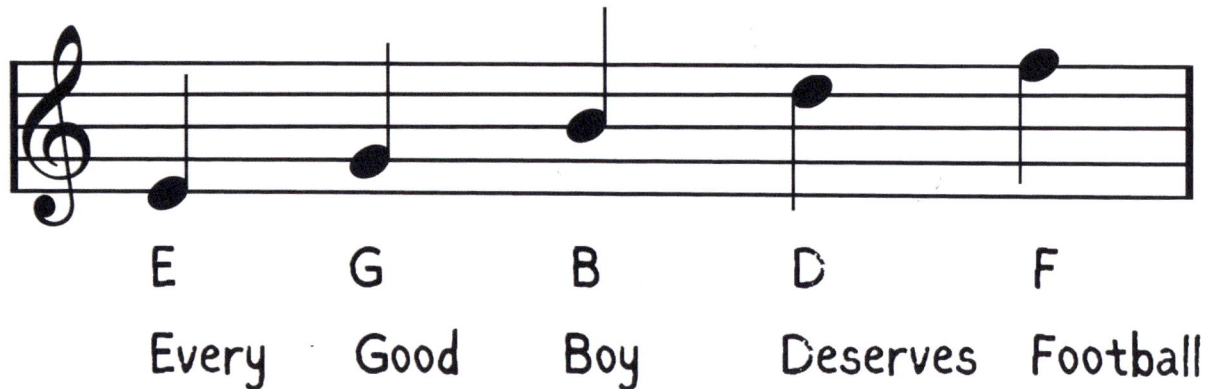

E	G	B	D	F
Every	Good	Boy	Deserves	Football

Treble Clef Notes
Space Rhymes With FACE

To help us remember the notes in the spaces, we can just remember the word FACE.

FACE for SPACE.

Write The Notes

Write the notes on the dotted lines. You don't have to do it all at once!

Don't forget, for the lines use:

Every Good Boy Deserves Football.

For the spaces use FACE.

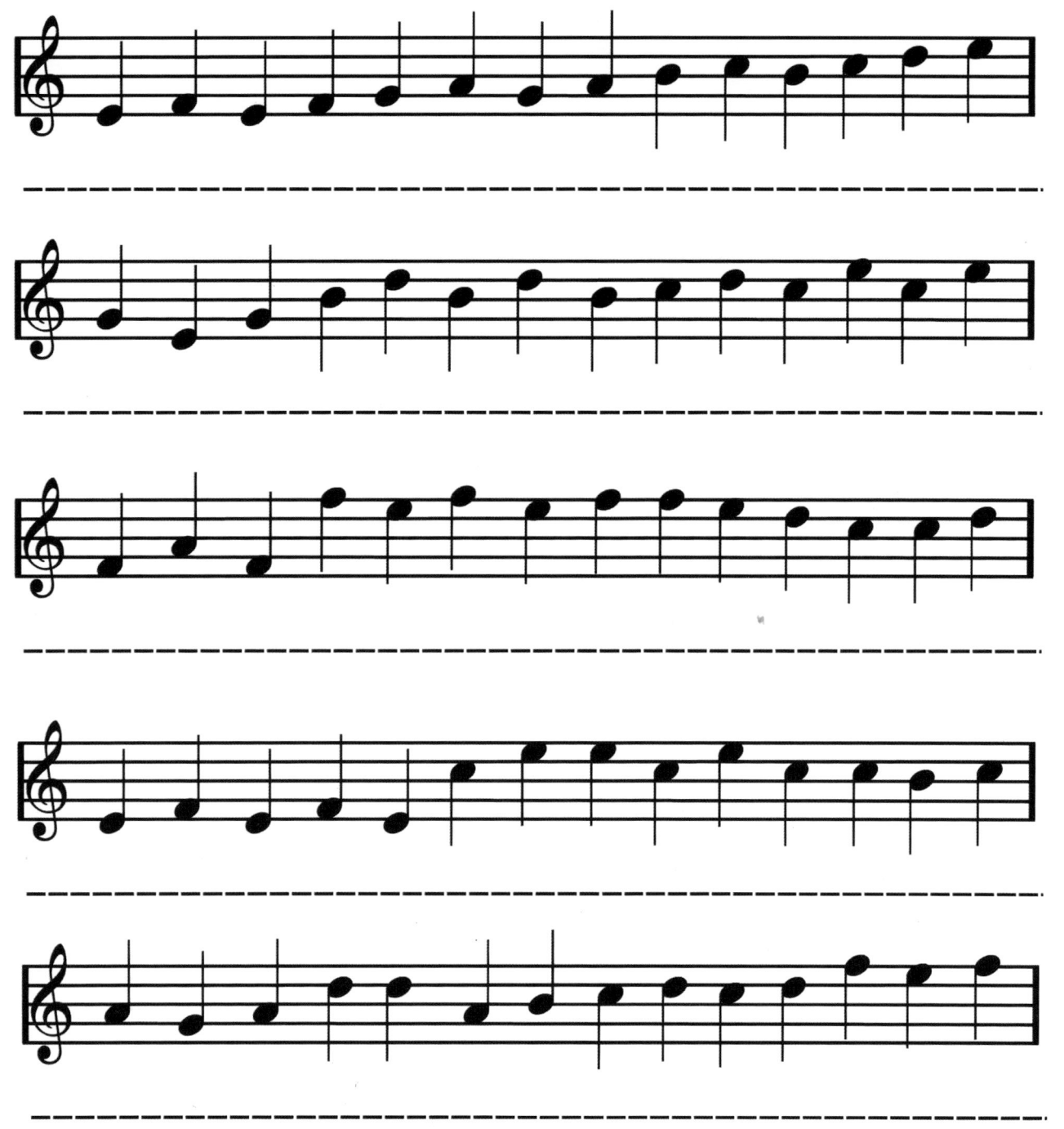

Bass Clef

Starting at A at the bottom, the notes go up in alphabetical order from each space to each line. These notes are lower in pitch than the notes on the treble clef until we get to middle C.

In the bass clef, middle C is one ledger line above the stave. It is the exact same note that is one ledger line below the stave in the treble clef.

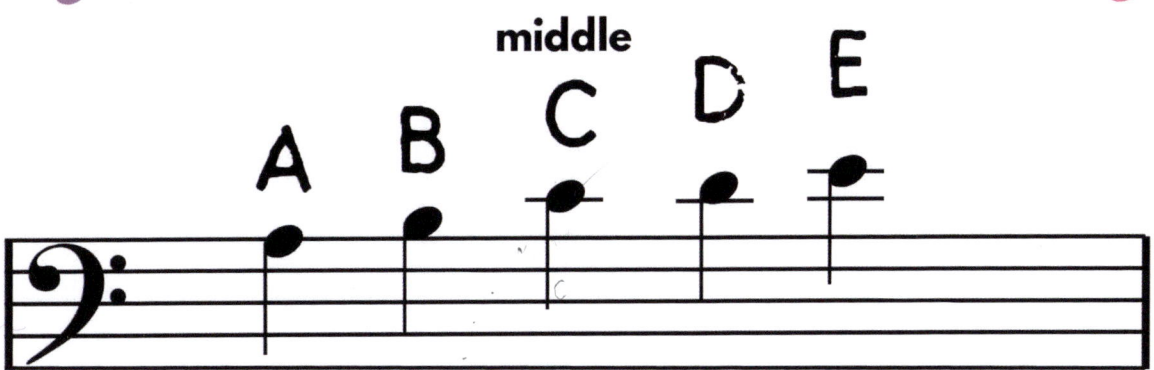

Below is the symbol for the bass clef.
Have a go at drawing some bass clefs below. Start by tracing the first ones.

8

Bass Clef Notes
The Rhyme For The Lines

To help us remember the notes on each line, we can learn the rhyme on the blackboard.

The letter at the beginning of each word is the note for each line, starting from the bottom to the top.

G	B	D	F	A

Grizzly	Bears	Don't	Frighten	Amy

Bass Clef Notes
The Rhyme For The Spaces

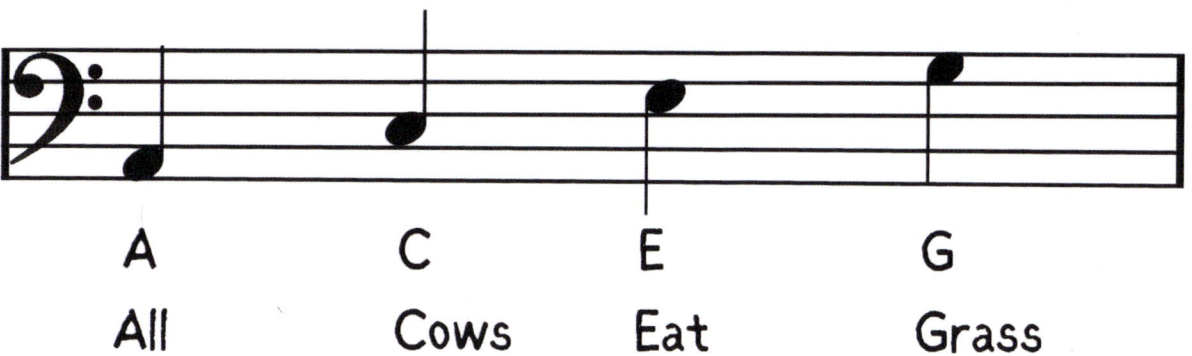

A — All
C — Cows
E — Eat
G — Grass

Write The Notes

Write the notes on the dotted lines.
Don't forget, for the lines use:
Grizzly Bears Don't Frighten Amy.
For the spaces use:
All Cows Eat Grass.

G B D E A E D B G A C E G

A G B A G E G A G A E A E

D A G E G A E D C B C C A

Notes Outside The Rhymes

We know each note goes up in alphabetical order from each line to each space, from A to G then starts again.

The notes above and below the stave are written on short lines called ledger lines, with spaces in between.

We work them out by continuing the alphabet from the notes we do know.

Or we can just learn them!

Here are useful ones to learn (I've included D and G in the treble clef and F and B in the bass, even though they're not ledger lines):

Treble Clef

Bass Clef

Write The Notes

Pay attention to the clef!

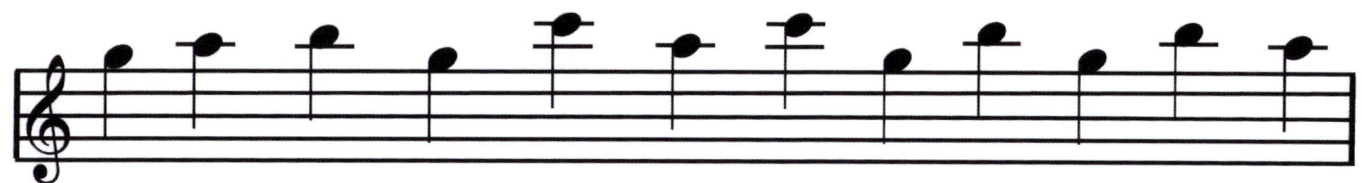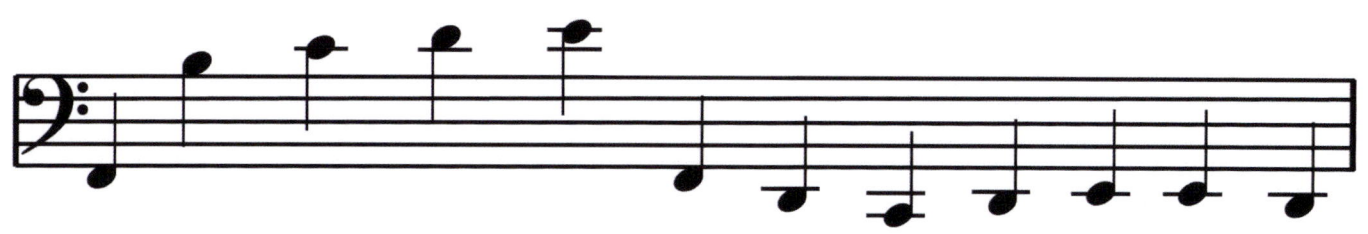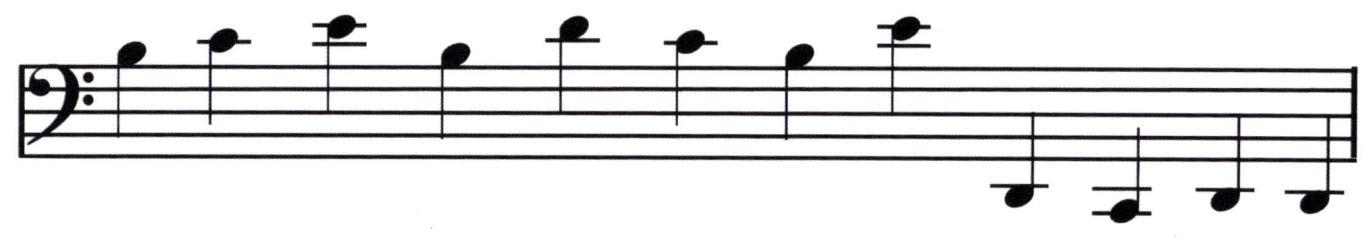

 # Note And Rest Length

In British English the notes have names and in American English they use the length of the note as its name.

In your exam you can use the British or the American names.

Here, each of the first 3 bars adds up to 4 crotchets.

Each of the second 3 bars adds up to 1 crotchet.

Quavers and semiquavers can be written separately or joined together.

Sometimes in music there are silences where we don't play or sing.
The length of time we are quiet for is shown by a "rest".
Each type of rest has a different length which we need to know.

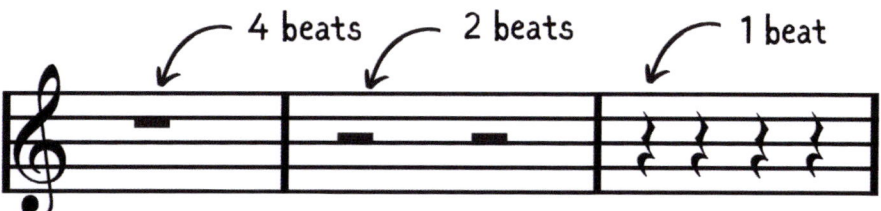

1 semibreve rest = 2 minim rests = 4 crotchet rests
1 whole rest = 2 half rests = 4 quarter rests

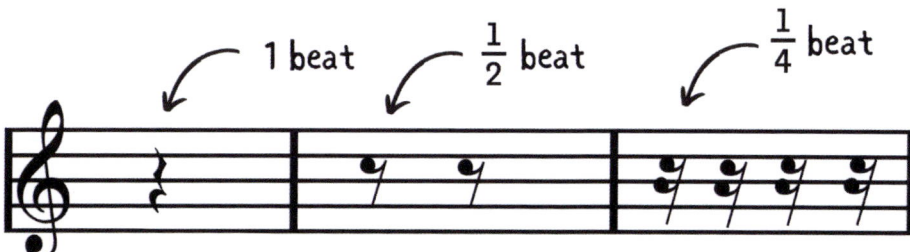

1 crotchet rest = 2 quaver rests = 4 semiquaver rests
1 quarter rest = 2 eighth rests = 4 sixteenth rests

Dotted Notes And Rests

When you see a dot next to a note or a rest, it means you ADD ON ANOTHER HALF of its value.

A semibreve lasts for 4 beats, so a dotted semibreve is 4 + 2 = 6 beats 𝐨.

A minim lasts for 2 beats, so a dotted minim is 2 + 1 = 3 beats 𝅗𝅥.

A crotchet lasts for 1 beat, so a dotted crotchet is $1 + \frac{1}{2} = 1\frac{1}{2}$ beats 𝅘𝅥.

A quaver lasts for $\frac{1}{2}$ a beat, so a dotted quaver is $\frac{1}{2} + \frac{1}{4} = \frac{3}{4}$ beats 𝅘𝅥𝅮.

These bars are NOT equal in length.

dotted semibreve	dotted minim	dotted crotchet	dotted quaver
6 beats	3 beats	$1\frac{1}{2}$ beats	$\frac{3}{4}$ beats

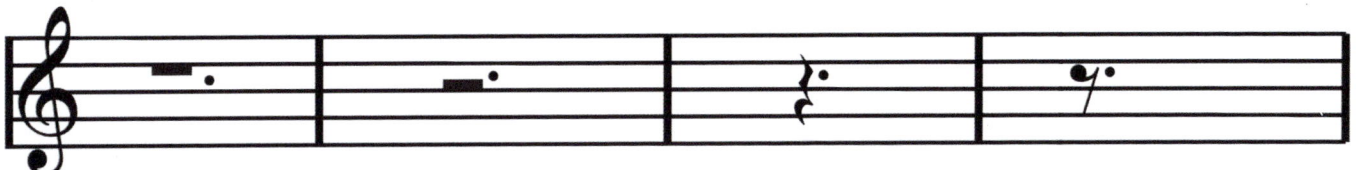

dotted semibreve rest	dotted minim rest	dotted crotchet rest	dotted quaver rest
6 beats	3 beats	$1\frac{1}{2}$ beats	$\frac{3}{4}$ beats

Draw The Notes

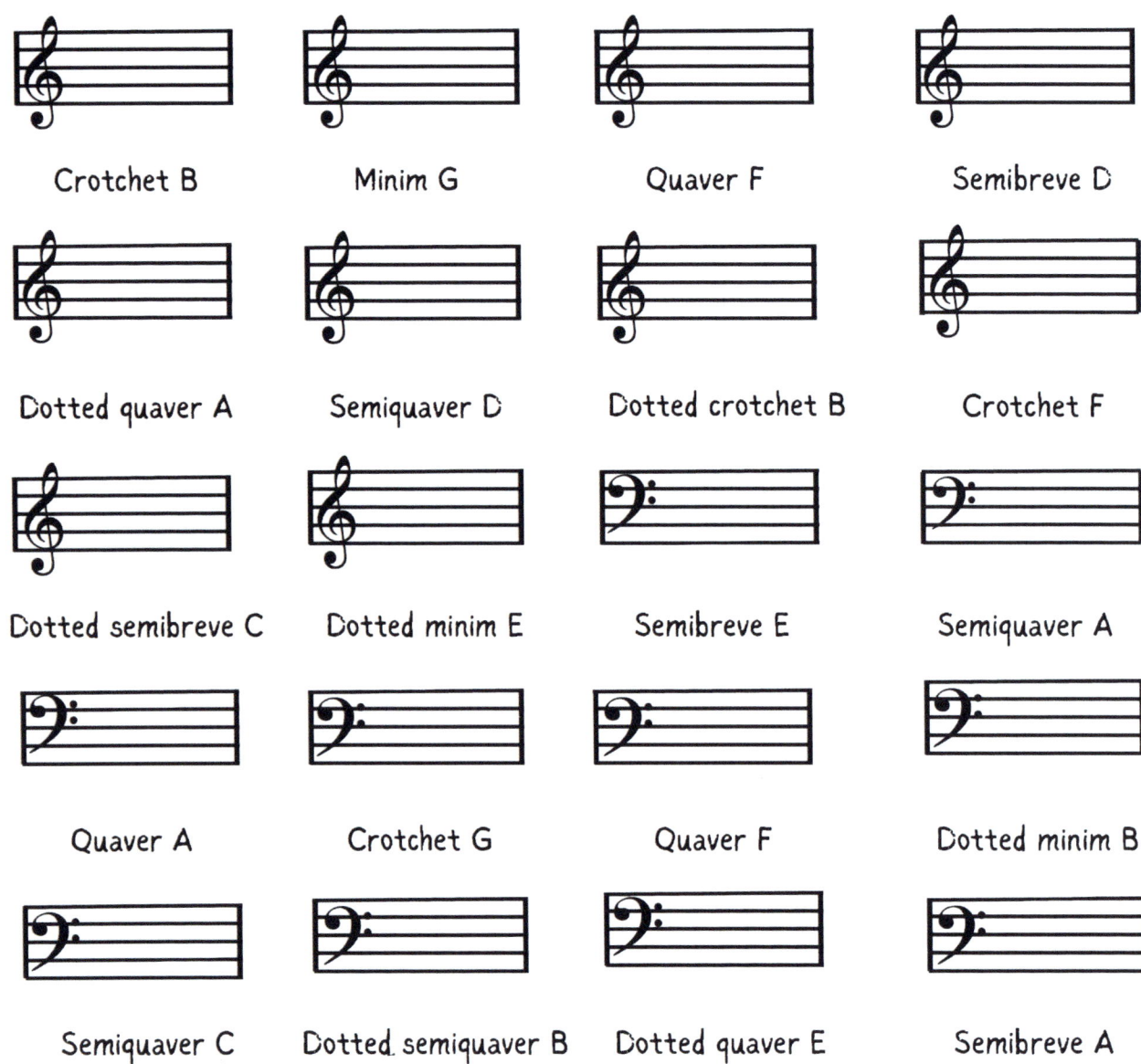

What Is The Note?
How Many Beats?

Eg A. 4 beats

Time Signatures

The time signature tells us how many beats are in each bar and how long each beat should last.

The top number is how many beats are in the bar.

The bottom number is how long the beat lasts.

For example:

2 on the bottom means each beat lasts for one minim.

4 on the bottom means each beat lasts for one crotchet.

8 on the bottom means each beat lasts for one quaver.

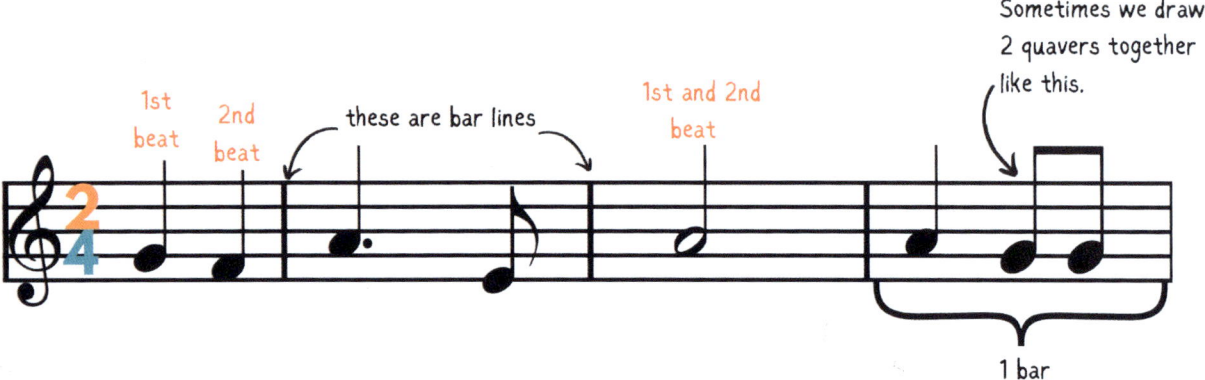

There are 2 beats in a bar and each beat lasts for 1 crotchet.

The notes and rests in each bar MUST add up to the same length as 2 crotchets.

23

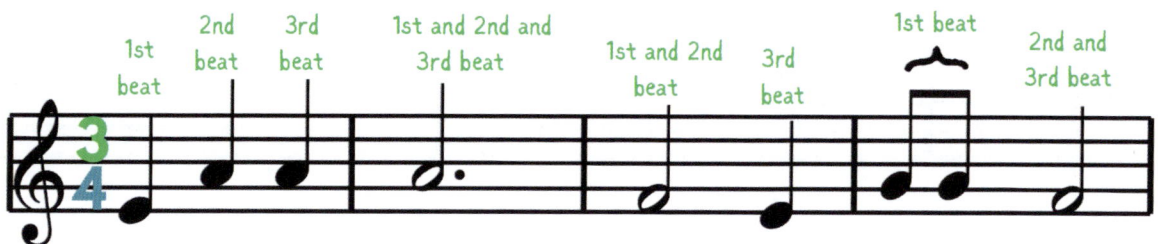

There are 3 beats in a bar and each beat lasts for 1 crotchet.

The notes and rests in each bar MUST add up to the same length as 3 crotchets.

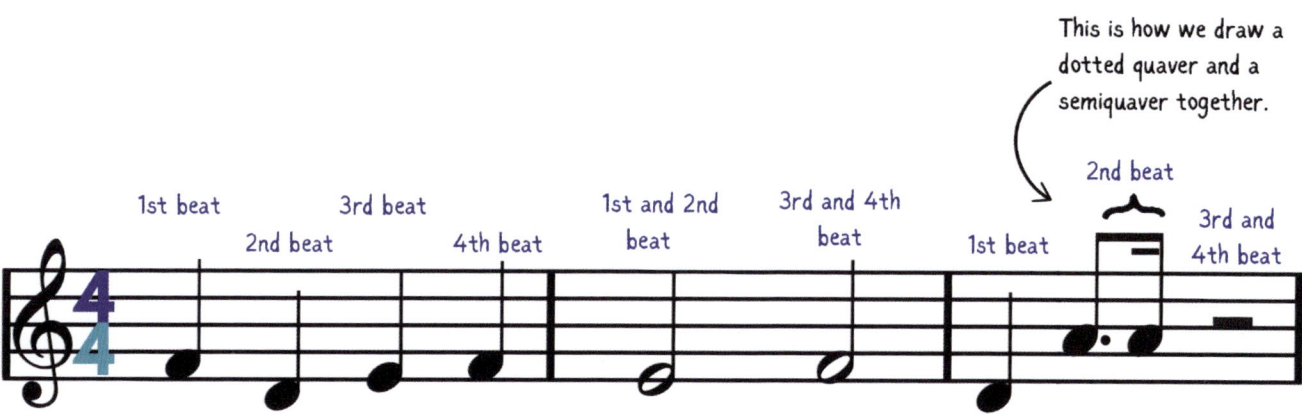

There are 4 beats in a bar and each beat lasts for 1 crotchet.

The notes and rests in each bar MUST add up to the same length as 4 crotchets.

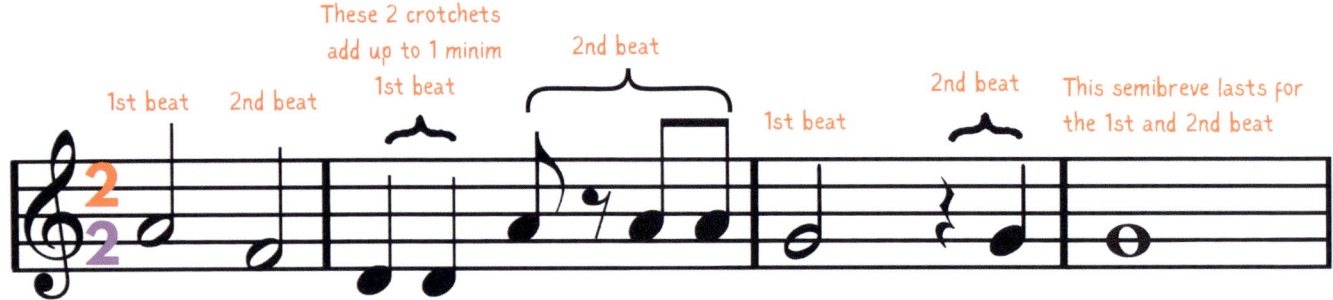

There are 2 beats in a bar and each beat lasts for 1 minim.

The notes and rests in each bar MUST add up to the same length as 2 minims.

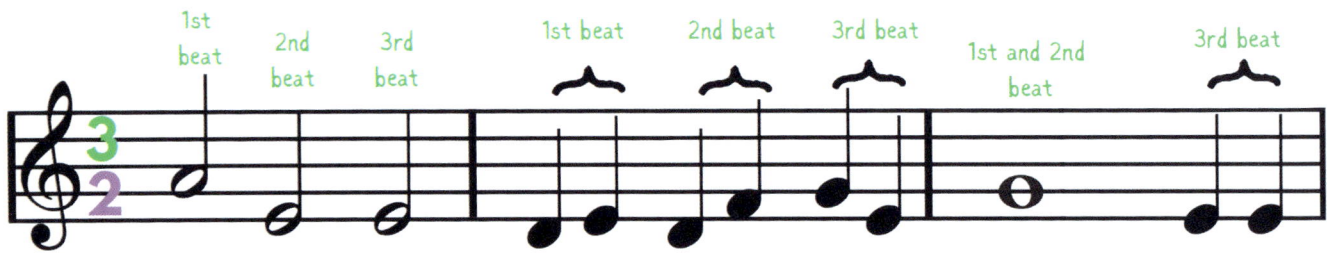

There are 3 beats in a bar and each beat lasts for 1 minim.

The notes and rests in each bar MUST add up to the same length as 3 minims.

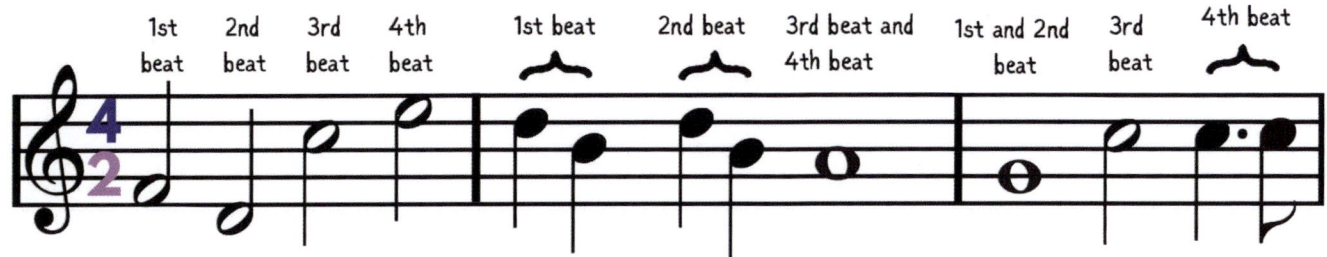

There are 4 beats in a bar and each beat lasts for 1 minim.

The notes and rests in each bar MUST add up to the same length as 4 minims.

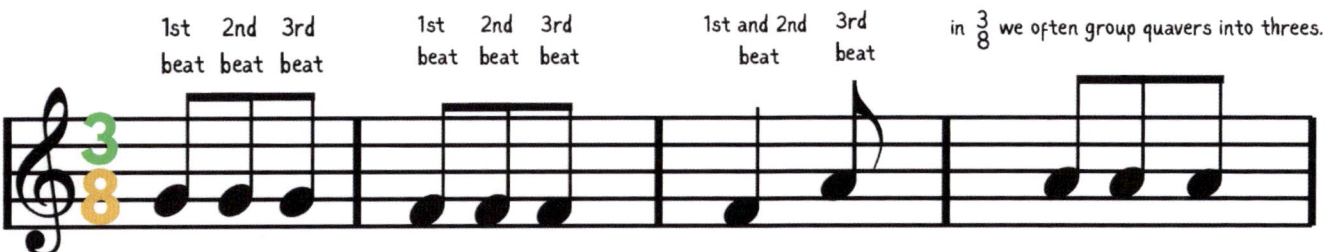

There are 3 beats in a bar and each beat lasts for 1 quaver.

The notes and rests in each bar MUST add up to the same length as 3 quavers.

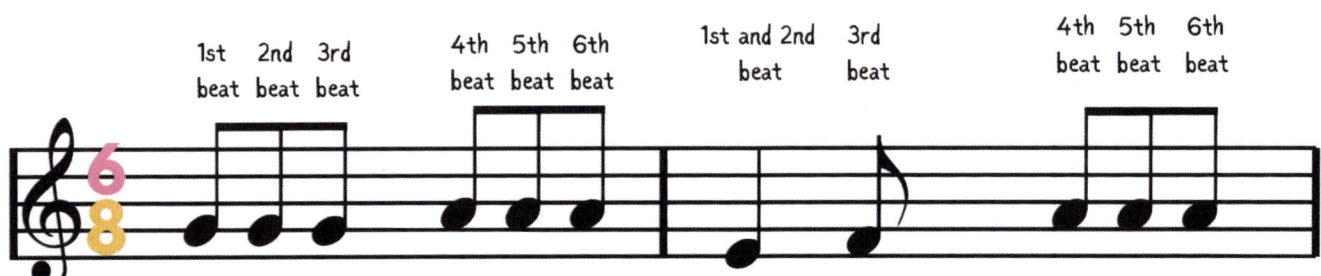

There are 6 beats in a bar and each beat lasts for 1 quaver.

The notes and rests in each bar MUST add up to the same length as 6 quavers.

Write The Time Signature

Fill in the time signatures. Remember, the top number is how many beats are in the bar. The bottom number is how long the beats are.

a)

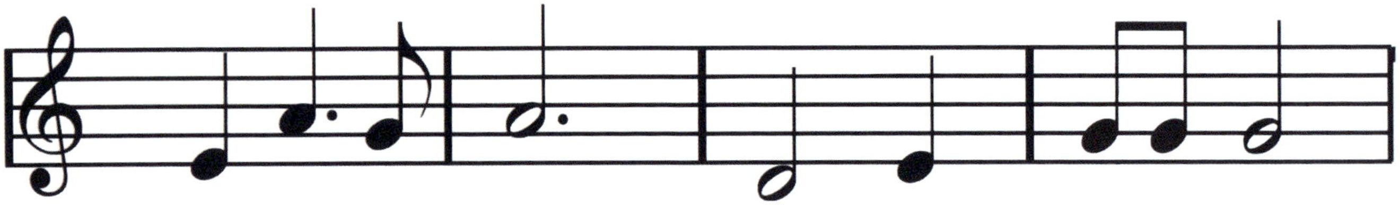

b)

c)

d)

e)

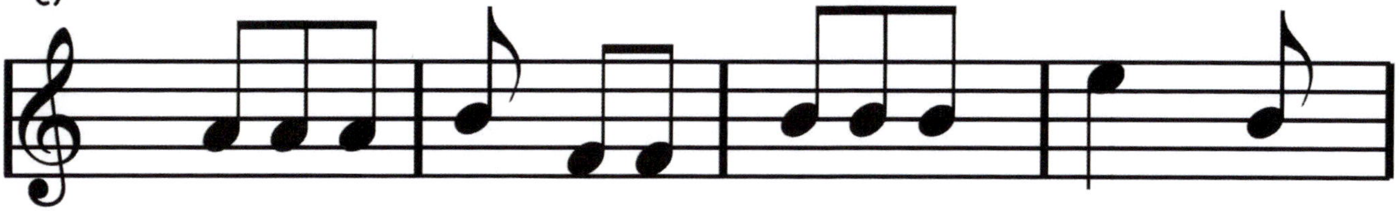

f)

g)

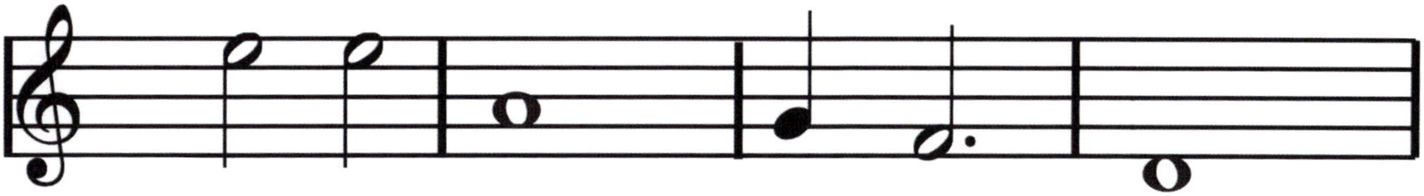

h)

Musical Terms

Here are some Italian terms used in music that you will need to know.

Instructions for playing (written above the music):

A tempo: in time

Adagio: slow

Allegretto: fairly quickly

Allegro: quick

Andante: at a walking pace

Moderato: at a moderate pace

Legato: smooth

Dolce: sweetly

Cantabile: in a singing style

Da Capo (DC): play again from the start

Things that change how you play (written throughout the music):

Crescendo (cresc.) means get louder.

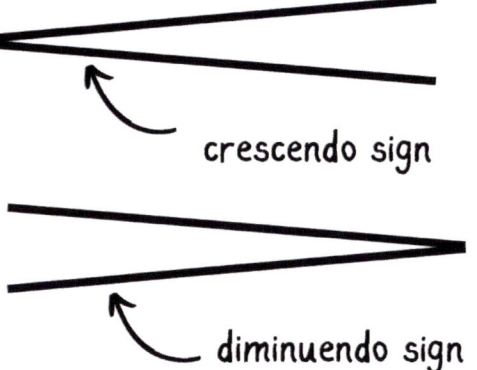

Decrescendo (decresc.) means get quieter.
Diminuendo (dim.) also means get quieter.

Accelerando (accel.) means gradually get faster.

Rallentando (rall.) means gradually slow down.
Ritardando (rit.) also means gradually slow down.

Staccato (stacc.) means to play the notes short and detached.

How loud? (written throughout the music):

Pianissimo (pp): very quiet pp

Piano (p): quiet p

Mezzo piano (mp): moderately quiet mp

Mezzo forte (mf): moderately loud mf

Forte (f): loud f

Fortissimo (ff): very loud ff

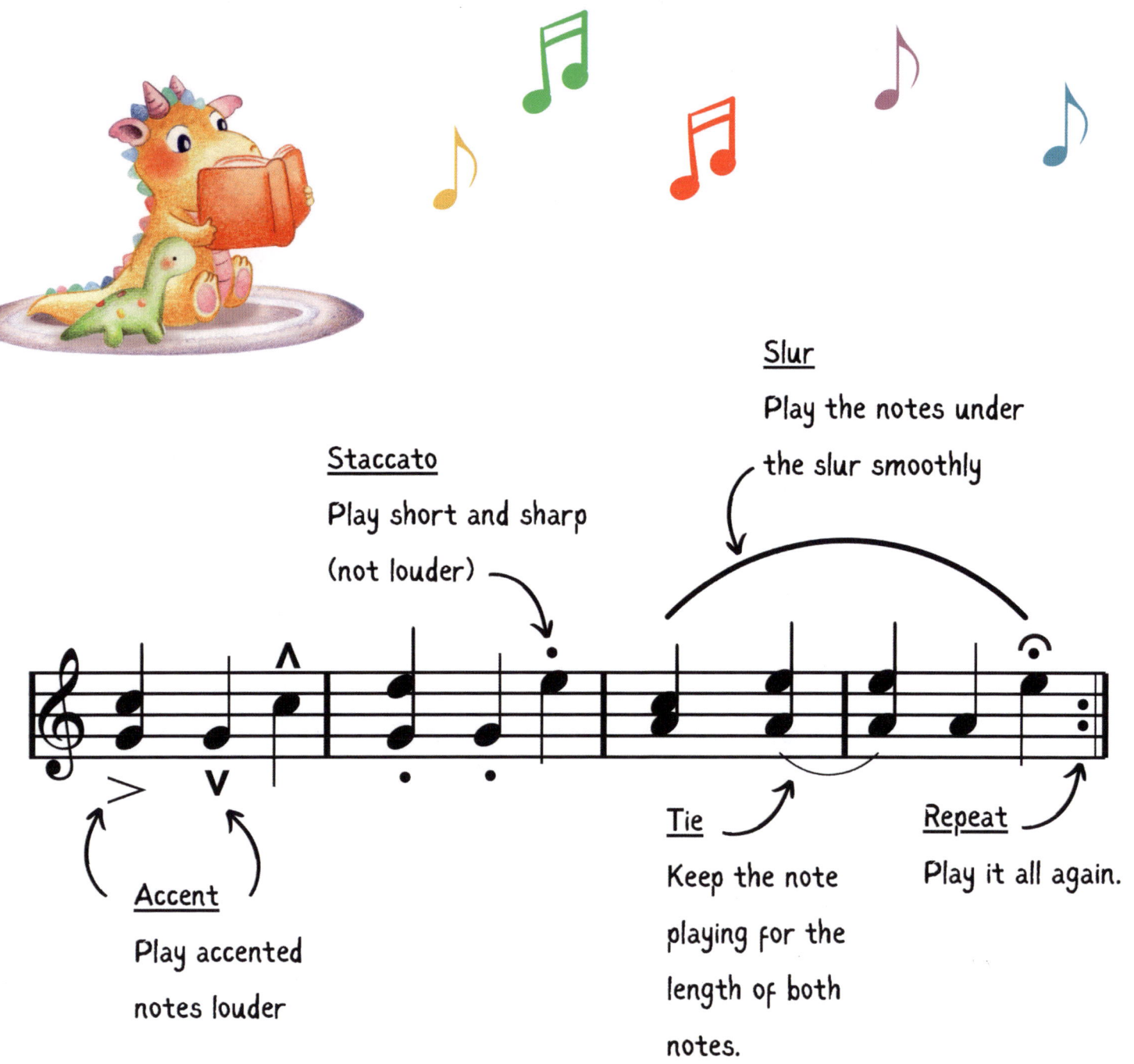

Answers

Page 5

E G B D F D B G E F A C E
B G E D F F C A A F E G E
C D A G E F G F E F E G F
F A F A B C D C B C E C D

Page 6

E F E F G A G A B C B C D E
G E G B D B D B C D C E C E
F A F F E F E F F E D C C D
E F E F E C E E C E C C B C
A G A D D A B C D C D F E F

Page 11

G B D F A A C E G
A G B C G E D A F
D A G F G A E B C

Page 12

G G G F F F D D D B B B B
A A C C E E G G E G E C A
D D G F G G A D D F A D A
G G B B G G G F F C D E F
D A G F G A E D C B C C A

Page 15

D D D C C C B B B A A A
G G G A A A B B B C C C
F F F E E E D D D C C C
B B B C C C D D D E E E

Page 16

D C B A D B A B C D B C
G A B G C A C G B G B A
F B C D E F D C D E E D
B C E B D C B E D C D D

33

Page 21. I've included all the versions of each note, as long as you have one of them, that's fine.

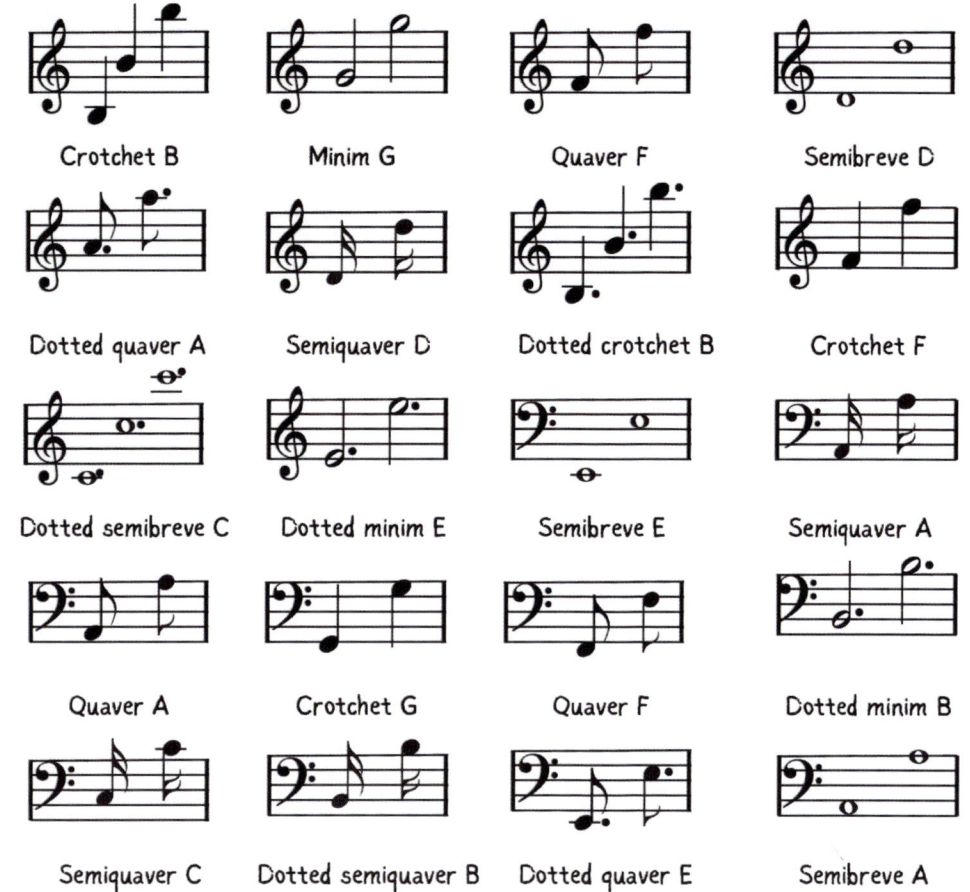

Page 22
(A4) F1 $\frac{1}{2}$ 2
D$\frac{3}{4}$ E2   B1$\frac{1}{2}$ 1
D6   1$\frac{1}{2}$ E3 $\frac{1}{4}$
G$\frac{1}{4}$ 4 $\frac{3}{4}$ E$\frac{1}{2}$
3   6   E4   B1

Page 27
a) $\frac{3}{4}$ b) $\frac{2}{4}$ c) $\frac{6}{8}$ d) $\frac{3}{2}$

Page 28
e) $\frac{3}{8}$ f) $\frac{4}{4}$ or $\frac{2}{2}$ g) $\frac{2}{2}$ or $\frac{4}{4}$ h) $\frac{3}{4}$

Please consider leaving me an Amazon review!

These are super important for independent authors. You can leave a review even if you purchased elsewhere.

Thanks in advance. Steph.

34

Other Books By Stephanie Lipsey-Liu

Check out Learn To Read Music For Beginners Book 2 to learn everything else you need to know to complete your ABRSM Grade 1 Theory.

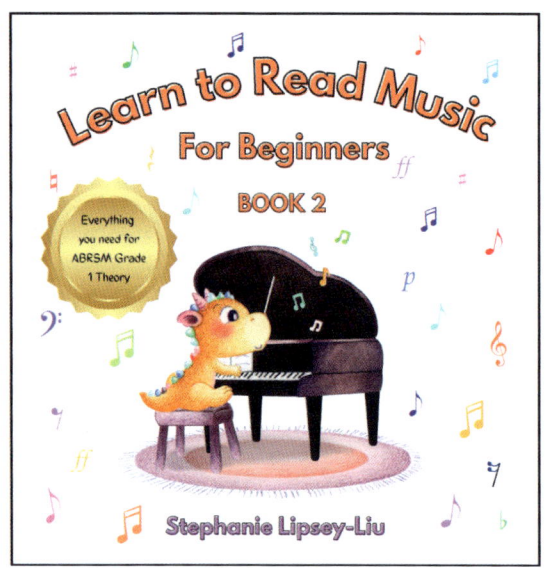

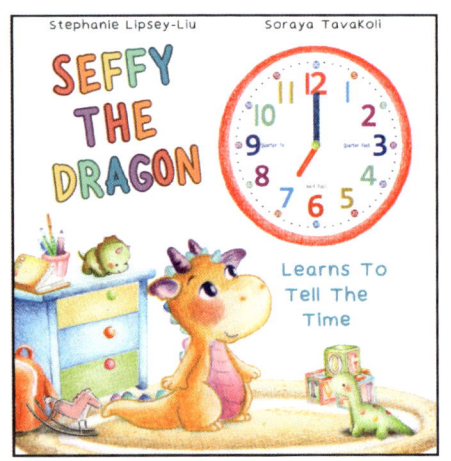
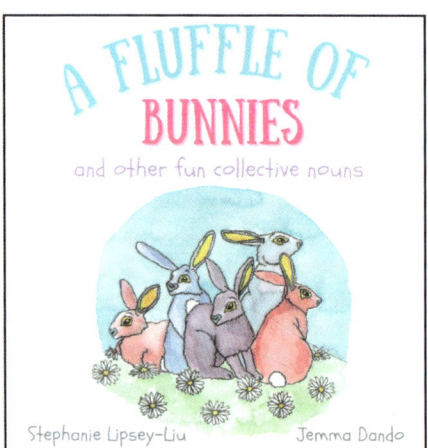

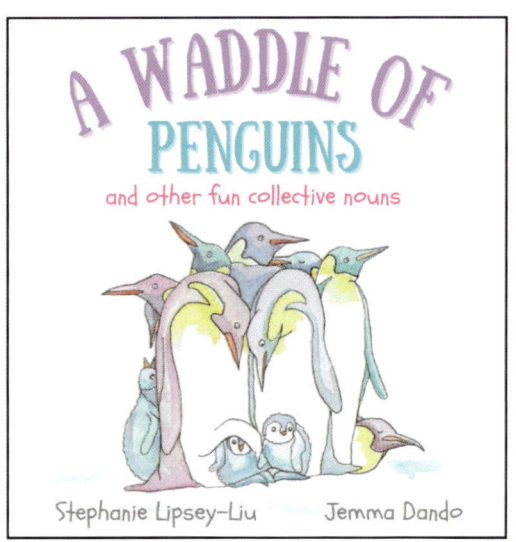

About The Author

Stephanie is an optician and children's author with a passion for music. She plays the piano to grade 7, the clarinet to grade 8 and completed her grade 5 theory. She is currently learning to play the harp. This book combines her passion for music and love of writing and she hopes to make it available to as many children as possible!

Printed in Great Britain
by Amazon